An Extraordinary Life

An Extraordinary Life

The Story of a Monarch Butterfly

by Laurence Pringle

Paintings by Bob Marstall

Orchard Books

NEW YORK

Orchard Books
A Grolier Company
95 Madison Avenue
New York, NY 10016

Manufactured in China
Printed by Toppan Printing Company, Inc.
Book design by Hans Teensma/Impress, Inc.

Hardcover 10 9 8 7 6 5 4
Paperback 10 9 8 7 6 5 4 3 2 1

Library of Congress Cataloging-in-Publication Data
Pringle, Laurence P.
An extraordinary life : the story of a monarch butterfly / by Laurence Pringle ;
paintings by Bob Marstall.
p. cm.
Includes bibliographical references (p.) and index.
Summary: Introduces the life cycle, feeding habits, migration, predators, and mating of the
monarch butterfly through the observation of one particular monarch named Danaus.
ISBN 0-531-30002-1 (tr.)   ISBN 0-531-33002-8 (lib. bdg.)   ISBN 0-531-07169-3 (pbk.)
1. Monarch butterfly—Juvenile literature. [1. Monarch butterfly. 2. Butterflies.]
I. Marstall, Bob, ill. II. Title.
QL561.D3P75 1997
595.78'9—dc20
96-31482

Acknowledgments

AN EXTRAORDINARY LIFE exists as a result of contributions from many people, beginning with editor Harold Underdown, who in the spring of 1993 suggested a book of this kind and was enthusiastic about the story of one monarch butterfly. For the most up-to-date information about monarchs we are grateful to Lincoln P. Brower of the University of Florida (who checked the manuscript for accuracy), Orley Taylor of the University of Kansas and Monarch Watch, Ken Brown of Monarch Watch, Robert Lederhouse of Michigan State University, David Gibo of the University of Toronto, Helen Ghiradella of the State University of New York at Albany, Bill Walton of the Monarch Migration Association of North America, Louise Zemaitis of the Cape May Bird Observatory, Fred Morrison of the Northampton Public Schools, and Bill Calvert of Texas Monarch Watch. Fred supplied caterpillars and also wisdom from his rich experience in raising monarchs; Bill was our invaluable guide at the Rosario monarch-wintering site in January 1995. We shared the Mexican adventure with Jaana Cutson, Ken and Molly Lindsay, Paul, Dulcie, Aaron, and Adam Lipman, Mary McDermott, Laurie Sanders, Ted Watt, Laura Wenk, and Faith Thayer. Special thanks to Faith—her enthusiasm and knowledge about monarchs contributed greatly to the Mexican trip and to this work. And thanks to Stephen Petegorsky for color transparencies of the full-page art. Special thanks to Diane de Groat for her invaluable and timely help.

Finally, we thank editors Melanie Kroupa and Maggie Herold and designer Hans Teensma for expertly guiding this book to completion.

—*Laurence Pringle and Bob Marstall*

To monarchs—only butterflies,
yet strong enough to lift the human heart
—L.P.

To my son, Christopher Buck Marstall,
whose sense of wonder will always inspire me
—B.M.

A Monarch Butterfly's Journey

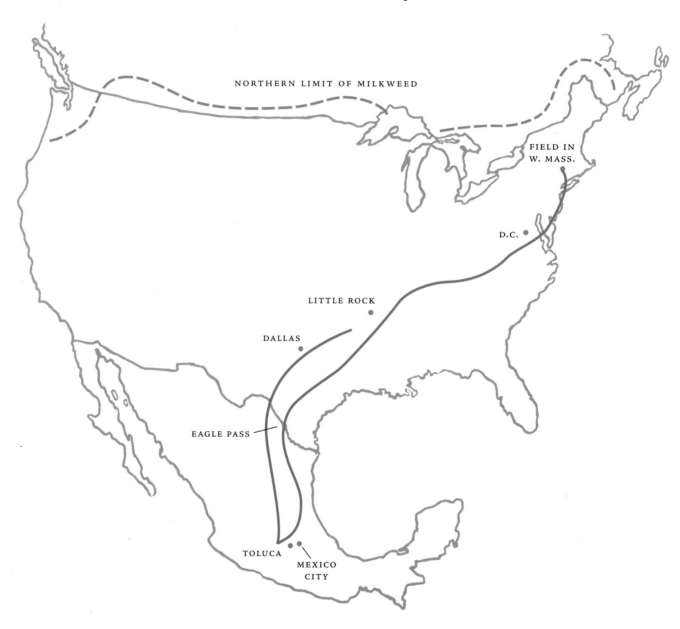

NORTHERN LIMIT OF MILKWEED

FIELD IN
W. MASS.

D.C.

LITTLE ROCK

DALLAS

EAGLE PASS

TOLUCA

MEXICO
CITY

Contents

OVERLEAF: *The story begins in late summer, in a Massachusetts hayfield.*

From a Massachusetts Hayfield

IT WAS A MOONLESS NIGHT in late August. Field crickets chirped in a Massachusetts hayfield. Their chorus was joined by tree crickets, and by katydids from the forest edge. The lush life of summer would soon be over, and the night-calling insects chirped and trilled insistently. They were engaged in the serious business of attracting mates and producing the next generation —the musicians that would play in the evening concerts of next summer.

The insect songs masked other night sounds: the footsteps of a fox hunting for mice; the tiny crackling sounds of a shrew gobbling down a beetle; and another, even tinier sound, as a monarch butterfly lost her grip on a milkweed leaf and fell dead in the hay.

She had lived just over a month as an adult. Yet in that time she had lived a full, rich life. She had flown over many acres of fields and gardens. She had sipped nectar from thousands of flowers. She had mated with a handsome male monarch. And then, providing for a

WHERE THE EGGS WERE LAID

mon·arch, noun—the ruler of a nation, such as an emperor or queen. When European colonists saw bright orange-and-black butterflies in North America, they were reminded of the prince of Orange, who became King William III of England, so they named the butterflies monarchs.

A monarch egg, enlarged about 30 times.

TOP OF PAGE: *Newly emerged monarch caterpillar compared in size with a United States nickel.*

new generation of monarchs, in the span of a few days she had laid more than four hundred eggs.

She had flown quickly, depositing each egg on a separate milkweed plant. The very last one was stuck to the underside of a leaf not far from where she fell. Like the rest, it was tiny—the size of a pinhead, but marked with a pattern of ridges like an exquisitely carved jewel. Like the rest, it contained the possibility of new life, and also of adventures far grander than the mother monarch had known.

Almost immediately, hints of the new life could be seen through the egg's translucent shell. Tiny dark spots moved within. They were the head and feet of a caterpillar—a very small caterpillar, just one twenty-fifth of an inch long. On the black dot that was its head, this caterpillar, or larva, had mouthparts that soon hardened into sharp cutting tools. They worked up and down, as human jaws do, but also cut from side to side.

Within a few days the caterpillar had rasped open a slit near the top of its egg. It wriggled free and promptly ate most of the empty eggshell. Then it grazed on downy hairs that grew from the leaf surface. Just a few hours after emerging from its egg, the caterpillar began to chew a hole through the leaf. It kept chewing and swallowing. The hole got bigger. So did the monarch caterpillar.

She was off to a good start. Not all of her mother's progeny had fared so well. Some of the four hundred eggs simply did not produce live caterpillars. A few eggs were eaten by insects that prowled milkweed plants looking for such morsels. Predatory insects and crab spiders also eat monarch larvae. Nevertheless, scores of other monarch caterpillars were still alive, chewing and growing, on the milkweed plants in the Massachusetts hayfield.

All over North America, in fact, monarch caterpillars were feeding on milkweed plants. More than a hundred species of milkweed grow in North America. The monarch is just one species of a whole group of butterflies—called Danaidae—that lay their eggs on these plants. So members of the Danaidae family are often called milkweed butterflies. With one exception, all milkweed butterflies live in or near the tropics. That exception—the species that lives and thrives far from the tropics and whose larvae feed on northern milkweed plants—is *Danaus plexippus*, the monarch butterfly.

Let's call this caterpillar, the one that emerged from her mother's last egg, Danaus.

At night Danaus stopped eating and rested. In fact, eating and resting was about all that she did. She grew larger. After just three days of life as a caterpillar, Danaus seemed about to burst out of her skin. Caterpillars and other insect larvae can do that. Of course their skins are not like human skin. Their skins are made of a tough, waterproof material called cuticle and are more like an outer skeleton (an exoskeleton). Danaus, like all insects, had no ribs, no backbone, not a bone in her body.

Danaus stopped eating and retreated to a sheltered place under a leaf. She gripped the leaf firmly. Beneath her tough outer skin another soft skin had formed, and now the two skins separated. Danaus pushed with her muscles and took in air, pressing outward against her old skin.

It split open along her back. Danaus rested, then wriggled and pushed some more. Her old skin split further, and at last she was able to raise her head free of it. Her struggles were not over. It took three hours, working and resting, for Danaus to molt completely. She emerged with a roomier outer skin that soon hardened. Her new skin was not only larger but also more colorful, ringed with black, white, and yellow.

A newly emerged caterpillar is called a first instar. After growing and molting its "skin," the caterpillar is called a second instar. A monarch caterpillar molts four times, becoming fully grown in its fifth instar stage.

Near the front and rear of a monarch caterpillar, a pair of slender black filaments wave in the air like tentacles. Do they help sense when danger is near? Do they help protect the caterpillar by warning enemies away? So far, no one knows.

A fully grown monarch caterpillar, shown about twice normal size.

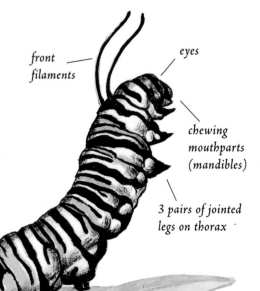

front filaments

eyes

chewing mouthparts (mandibles)

3 pairs of jointed legs on thorax

rear filaments

5 pairs of fleshy prolegs on abdomen

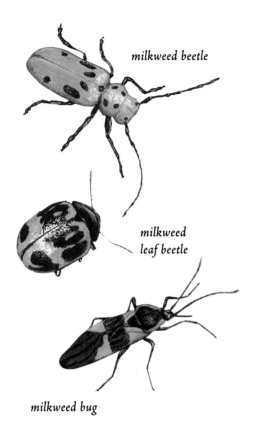

milkweed beetle

milkweed leaf beetle

milkweed bug

Milkweed plants contain a sticky white sap. In some kinds of milkweed the sap is poisonous. (The poisons are cardiac glycosides — heart poisons.) Beetles, milkweed bugs, and monarch caterpillars avoid eating much of the sap but usually have some of the poison in their bodies. Their bright colors are a "poison" warning to birds and other predators.

Before beginning to munch on milkweed, Danaus ate her cast-off old skin, which was full of proteins—nutrients she would need as she continued to grow. A monarch larva usually molts every three or four days, molting four times before reaching full size. Each time Danaus molted, her new skin had larger black, white, and yellow rings. After three molts Danaus was about an inch long. Her appetite also grew. Instead of eating holes in leaves, she now kept chewing until she ate most of an entire milkweed leaf, then moved on to another.

One day Danaus ate the last leaf on her milkweed stem. Still hungry, she walked headfirst down the plant stalk and set off across the field, searching for more milkweed. Fortunately, milkweeds were plentiful. After a farmer had mowed the field in June, new growth from deep milkweed roots had soon sprouted and now rose above the new crop of hay. A clump of tall plants loomed ahead of Danaus. She walked to the bottom of one stem and touched her mouth to it, sensing milkweed. Danaus climbed the stem and began to eat.

She was not the only insect in this clump of milkweed. Red milkweed beetles and milkweed leaf beetles also munched on the leaves. Like Danaus, these beetles usually nipped through leaf veins before beginning to feed in an area. From the cuts oozed a sticky white fluid called latex. It looked like milk; this fluid is the source of milkweed's name. However, the "milk" of milkweed contains a kind of poison. By cutting off the flow of latex to parts of a leaf, the beetles and Danaus could then eat those parts without taking in much of the milk.

The bitter taste of this white fluid discourages many kinds of insects from ever eating milkweed. In fact, some newly emerged monarch caterpillars even drown in this milk or get stuck in it when they accidentally chew through a leaf vein and release a flow of latex.

assassin bug

Both assassin and ambush bugs may pounce on monarch caterpillars. In Texas and other southern states, monarch eggs and small caterpillars may be eaten by fire ants.

Danaus was now big enough to chew quickly through the base of a leaf's main stem, or petiole, reducing the flow of the bitter milk to the whole leaf. She ate most of the leaf. It was early evening, so she climbed farther up the stem, seeking a higher leaf to sleep under. She passed by a partly eaten leaf. With her weak eyesight Danaus didn't notice a grim scene just inches away. Another monarch caterpillar lay on the leaf surface, but it wasn't moving. An assassin bug crouched by its body. The assassin bug had pierced the caterpillar's skin with its beak and injected saliva that first paralyzed its prey, then changed the caterpillar's tissues to liquid. The predatory bug had begun to sip its liquid meal.

Danaus had nothing to fear from this assassin bug. It would feast for hours on the other caterpillar, and this meal would satisfy its hunger for a week or more. Assassin bugs and stinkbugs had killed other monarch larvae in the milkweed-studded hayfield. Tachina flies had also laid eggs on some caterpillars, from which hatched parasitic larvae that nourished themselves within the bodies of caterpillars—and killed them in the process. Still, scores of other monarch caterpillars survived, eating milkweed and growing.

catbird

One day a huge gray form suddenly appeared near Danaus. A catbird fixed its sharp brown-eyed gaze on her. One swift peck and her life would end. But the catbird flew off and soon spied a green caterpillar that it promptly ate. Other birds also seemed to avoid eating monarch caterpillars and the beetles living on milkweed. The bright colors of the beetles and the caterpillars seemed to act like a warning: "Watch out—we eat milkweed and we taste bad!"

With its rear prolegs grasping the silk mat, the caterpillar hangs head down. The front of its body curves up, forming a J shape. (Caterpillar shown about twice normal size.)

After Danaus molted for the last time, her new body measured two inches long. She was gorgeous in glossy black and bright white and yellow. In just two weeks she had multiplied her weight more than twenty-five hundred times. Still she continued to eat and rest, eat and rest, storing food and energy for the next stage of her life. Each molt had been a struggle that brought a dramatic change in her body. Now she was ready for a greater struggle, and the most dramatic change of all. Danaus climbed down from the milkweed plant and explored across the hay. She found a sturdy hay stem that formed an arch a few inches above the ground. Holding fast to it, she began swaying her head from side to side, spewing a line of silk from a gland beneath her mouth and weaving a dense mat of silk on the stem's surface. After a rest, she twisted around so that tiny hooks on her rear pair of legs, at the end of her abdomen, could grasp the silk mat. Slowly she let go of the stem with her other legs. Her body swung free. Now she hung head down from the stem.

Danaus hung there motionless for several hours. Her bright colors faded and a bluish green tinge shone through her skin. Then she began the familiar routine of molting—pushing, wriggling, taking in air, pumping blood, pressing outward against her old skin. It split just in back of her head, then began to open down her back.

Clearly this was not just another molt. What emerged from her old skin was not a new, bigger larval skin but a glistening yellow-green form. Her old skin split further and shrank upward. It still clung to the silk mat on the stem, but Danaus the caterpillar had disappeared. She was now a chrysalis.

Danaus still clung to the stem by the feet of her old skin, which had shriveled up by the silk mat, like a pair of pants around a person's ankles. The outer surface of the chrysalis had not yet hardened, and Danaus had one vital job to do before that happened. A black stalk called a cremaster had developed within her body when she was a caterpillar. A knob on the end of the cremaster was covered with scores of tiny hooks facing in all directions. Danaus had to twist the knob of the cremaster to snag the hooks on to the silk mat so that her chrysalis would be firmly stuck to the stem. If she failed, the legs of her old skin would soon dry up and let go of the mat. She would fall to the ground and lie there helpless, with no chance of emerging successfully as a butterfly.

Still head down and sightless, Danaus used her muscles to twist the cremaster up around her old skin. She pushed it up toward the stem. There! She felt the knob hook on to the silk! For a moment she swiveled violently, driving more of the cremaster's hooks into the mat. Then she stopped moving. The walls of her chrysalis slowly hardened around her.

Held to the stem by its strong black stalk, the chrysalis looked like a jade jewel studded with tiny gold gems. It hung motionless and well camouflaged among the stems and leaves of the hayfield.

A monarch butterfly develops within its chrysalis over a span of five to fifteen days, depending on the temperature. Danaus's mother had been a midsummer pupa; for her the pupation process had lasted just nine days. But now summer was nearly over. The days grew shorter. Some nights were cool enough to chill the crickets and katydids, slowing their calls. The cool temperatures slowed the pace of change within Danaus's chrysalis.

Nevertheless, within twelve days she had changed dramatically: from a creature that walked on sixteen legs and ate leaves to one that would fly on four wings and sip liquids from flowers. Her trusty cutting mouthparts were replaced by a hollow drinking tube. Her caterpillar digestive system that had broken down thousands of milkweed bites was no longer needed. It was replaced by a much smaller and

The old skin first splits open at the bottom (head) end. As the split widens, a butterfly pupa wriggles free of its old caterpillar skin.

The cremaster stalk of the pupa holds it firmly to the silk mat spun by the caterpillar.

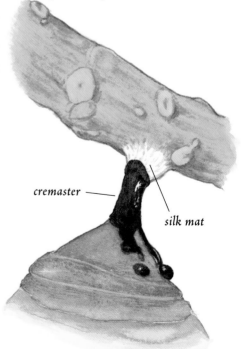

cremaster

silk mat

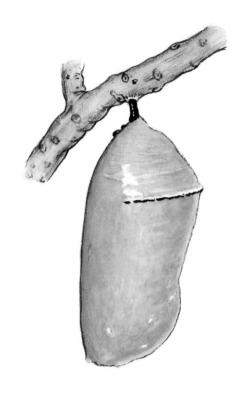

The pupa must shed all of its old caterpillar skin in order to develop into a healthy butterfly.

Its caterpillar skin discarded, the pupa soon stops quivering, and its chrysalis skin hardens.

The chrysalis hangs motionless for five to fifteen days. (Chrysalis drawn about twice normal size.)

People have wondered why flecks of gold mark the green surface of the chrysalis. They are always in specific places on its surface. Some scientists believe that the gold spots help hide the chrysalis from birds or other creatures that might eat it. Like drops of dew that reflect sunlight, they make the true form of the chrysalis hard to see.

simpler system that would enable her to digest flower nectar.

While these remarkable changes occurred, the chrysalis hung from the stem, not moving. It began to slowly lose its green color, however, and by the tenth day the chrysalis was black and dark orange. Actually the chrysalis skin itself was almost transparent, and the pattern of black and orange—with flecks of white—showing through was the body and wings of Danaus, almost ready to begin her life as a monarch butterfly.

A cold weather front passed over New England. Danaus stayed snug in her shelter as raindrops dripped from the hard, smooth surface of the chrysalis. Then, on the eve of her fourteenth day within her chrysalis, warm air from the south swept over Massachusetts. The crickets and katydids called with renewed vigor. Though it was late September, dawn brought a sunny, summerlike day.

The butterfly's colors show through the skin of the chrysalis.

Once the chrysalis skin splits open by the butterfly's head, it soon fractures in six other places.

In just a few minutes, the whole butterfly is free of the chrysalis.

A silvery frosted look spread over the chrysalis—a sign that Danaus's body was separating from its outer shell. The chrysalis shook as Danaus began to move, and a crack appeared at the bottom, by her head. A slender black leg emerged, then another. Within a few seconds the chrysalis split further and most of Danaus—head, legs, and short, stumpy wings—burst into view, into the light and air.

Danaus wrenched her abdomen loose from the chrysalis, then clung to the remains of the chrysalis and the stem with her new legs. She had needed only a minute to break free, but now she was weak and still unable to fly. She began to pump blood from her abdomen into her wings. As her abdomen shrank, her wings expanded and then gradually hardened.

Her antennae hardened, too. Danaus waved them in the air, detecting scents of plants, learning about her surroundings. She

As body fluid is pumped into the wings, they expand to their maximum size in about fifteen minutes. About two hours must pass before the wings are firm enough for flight.

began to uncoil and then recoil the two halves of her drinking tube, or proboscis. They had developed separately and had to be uncoiled and pressed together to lock into a single workable tube. Her proboscis seemed to work fine, so Danaus left it coiled under her head. Meanwhile, she continued to pump blood into her wings, pausing briefly to rest.

Her wings unfolded, grew larger, flattened. They rose straight above her back. Only the undersides of her wings showed—black and tan with white spots. Each front wing measured two inches across. They had reached their full size but were still soft. Danaus waited. Two hours would pass before her wings were hard enough for flight. She helped the process by walking a short distance up the hay stem, into more direct sunlight. She flexed her new wing muscles, opening and closing her wings. The bright orange, black, and white of her wing tops shone in the sun.

As a caterpillar Danaus had had six simple eyes that could barely make out areas of light and shadow. Now she scanned her surroundings with eyes made up of thousands of tiny lenses. She could see the hay and milkweed plants around her. Her antennae detected the scent of flowers.

Without thought, without practice, Danaus gave her wings a powerful downstroke. Her feet lifted off of the stem. She was moving up, up through the air. She began to explore the world as a butterfly.

Across a Continent

DANAUS WAS HUNGRY. Within her chrysalis she had lived on energy reserves from her milkweed-eating days. Now she hunted for a source of sweet flower nectar.

She flew and glided over scores of milkweeds in the hayfield. They still offered plenty of leaves for caterpillars, but their flowering time was past. The milkweed blossoms had developed into rough-coated pods packed tight with dark brown seeds attached to white plumes. Some of the pods had split open. The sun dried the outermost plumes into fluffy parachutes that the wind freed and carried away, each bearing its cargo of a milkweed seed.

Danaus spied yellow and purple flowers at the edge of the hayfield. She sipped nectar from goldenrod, then from New England asters—roadside "weeds" that were a bountiful garden for many insects but especially for Danaus and other monarchs who joined her. The nearby milkweed had yielded a fine crop of butterflies, both males and females.

FROM MASSACHUSETTS
TO THE RIO GRANDE

During World War II, schoolchildren across America collected twenty-five million pounds of milkweed pods. The lightweight plumes inside the pods were used to fill navy life preservers.

alar scent glands

male
(actual size)

Male and female monarchs look almost identical. The black veins in male wings have narrow black borders, so they appear to be a bit thinner than the veins of female wings. Males have a black spot on a vein on the upper surface of each rear wing. These spots are more than a decoration; they are scent glands that may lure females during mating time.

However, Danaus and the other monarchs were the last generation of the year. In nearly all ways they were exactly like monarchs born in the summer, but their reproductive systems were not fully developed. Although the monarchs perched close to one another as they feasted on flower nectar, they showed no interest in mating. In the late afternoon an autumn chill crept over the wildflowers. One by one the monarchs flew off. Danaus flew to a chokecherry tree in a hedgerow and slept there, hanging upside down under a leaf.

Danaus had picked a resting place that faced southeast, where

cleome

zinnia

marigold

the first rays of the morning sun would fall. After dawn she walked to the top of the leaf and waited for the sun to warm her body. A monarch cannot fly until the temperature of its wing muscles, within its thorax, reaches about fifty-five degrees Fahrenheit (thirteen degrees Celsius). Danaus spread her wings, basking in the sun. When she felt warm enough, she beat her wings a few times and glided to feed again on the roadside goldenrods and asters.

After drinking her fill, Danaus flew up—a hundred feet or more—higher than she had ever flown. She flew over a forest. The milkweed-studded hayfield that had been her nursery and her only home vanished from sight. Danaus flew a few miles, then glided down to investigate a mass of flowering plants in a backyard. There were zinnias, marigolds, phlox. She moved quickly from one blossom to another, sipping nectar.

This garden, as well as other gardens, fields, and roadsides in the

female
(actual size)

sunflower

cosmos

phlox

*mourning cloak butterfly
(about actual size)*

*Unlike monarchs, most butterflies
of the United States and Canada
survive the winter as chrysalides.
A few species, including the mourning
cloak butterfly, live through winter as
adults. They hibernate in tree holes,
under loose tree bark, or in other
shelter, then emerge early in
the spring.*

area, was rich with flowering plants—a butterfly paradise. But Danaus did not linger. Refueled, she took flight again. Something within her told her to keep moving, and to keep moving south.

That something was Danaus's "brain." Compared with a person or even with a mouse, Danaus did not have much of a brain. It was just a concentration of nerve cells about the size of a pinhead, properly called a cerebral ganglion. Danaus could not think or reason, but within her ganglion were stored bits of information that were vital for a monarch butterfly living in Massachusetts in the early autumn. All across the United States and in southern Canada, monarchs by the millions were responding to the butterfly wisdom stored in their ganglia: fly south. Monarchs are tropical butterflies, and lingering in the north would bring certain death with the first hard frost.

The ganglion in Danaus's head also helped guide her way and gave her information about long-distance traveling. Compared with migratory birds, a monarch is not an especially strong flyer, but it is a smart flyer. It takes advantage of favorable winds and other conditions that help it on its journey. Danaus soon had an opportunity to use some of the information in her ganglion. Flying south over fields and homes, she felt warm air rising all around her. This was a thermal—a spiraling mass of air warmed by the land surface. Thermals can be large or small. The dark surface of a parking lot, absorbing solar energy, can warm the air above it and create a thermal. Danaus had found a big one. She took advantage of it, flying higher and higher, letting the warm air carry her a half mile into the sky. She spiraled up, occasionally flapping her wings, gaining altitude while using very little energy.

Danaus then began to fly south. When she reached cooler air at the edge of the thermal, she began to descend gradually. Before long she caught another thermal and rose higher. She gained mile after mile, gliding along with occasional wingbeats. Far below Danaus the landscape changed. Sunlight glared from a huge body of water: Long Island Sound. It still held warmth from the summer sun, and Danaus felt the lift of rising air under her wings. She crossed fifteen miles of water easily. By late afternoon, when she settled down in a Long Island pine tree for the night, she had gained eighty miles for the day. Several other monarchs also slept in the pine.

The next morning Danaus found phlox, cosmos, and other flowers in a garden. She fluttered from blossom to blossom, sucking up nectar, not knowing that this garden was a dangerous place for butterflies. Here a house cat often lurked among the flowers. After years of failure it seldom tried to catch birds, but it had had success with butterflies. Even now it lay partly hidden among the phlox stems with a smashed spicebush swallowtail butterfly under one paw.

Danaus landed on a flower head above the cat. It crouched, then sprang toward her. Danaus saw the movement, the huge shape hurtling in her direction. She had time for one strong downbeat of her wings. She rose, escaped. In another split second the cat crashed back into the flowers, and Danaus was heading south out of the garden. One cat claw had ripped the edge of her hind wing.

A monarch butterfly is not a fragile creature. It has a sturdy

A monarch butterfly's body is covered with tiny, protective scales. They vary in size, shape, and color, depending on where they occur. Over a million scales cover a monarch's wings. This close-up view shows scales from a wing top, 25 times larger than actual size.

Strong winds may push migrating monarchs off course. Migrants have landed in Bermuda, on the Caribbean islands, and on ships far out in the Atlantic. Monarchs do not fly at night. Those that are far from land must find a resting place; they have even landed on offshore oil rigs in the Gulf of Mexico.

thorax, where its powerful wing muscles are attached. The wings themselves are covered with tiny overlapping scales like shingles on a roof and are surprisingly tough. However, a monarch weighs just one-fiftieth of an ounce, about half a gram. (It takes five monarchs to equal the weight of a United States penny.) Wind can push a migrating monarch far off course. Wind can also delay a monarch on its journey.

Danaus had benefited from perfect flying conditions, but now the weather changed. Strong winds from the west forced her to fly low as she crossed Long Island. She passed over fields, houses, highways, and forests, rising higher when she had to but usually staying within fifty feet of the ground. In the afternoon she flew over a bay. The full force of the wind swept across the open water and blew Danaus eastward. She struggled to gain a few miles to the south. When she finally reached the barrier island of sand south of Long Island, Danaus had little energy left. She found a patch of seaside goldenrod and joined other monarchs there. They rested and sipped nectar.

Jostled by the wind, stung by blowing sand, the monarchs clung to goldenrod flowers all through the night. The morning brought no relief. Despite the wind, after drinking her fill Danaus set off to the southwest. She flew over the surf, then out over the Atlantic, keeping a few feet above the ocean waves.

A fierce gust of wind slammed her down just as a wave rose beneath her. She was in the water! With all her strength she beat her wings again and again and lifted off the surface before she was drenched. Danaus turned and headed back to shore. The wind drove her a mile eastward before she settled down on another clump of seaside goldenrod.

The winds calmed at night. Next morning, after basking in the sun and drinking more nectar, Danaus and scores of other monarchs, pushed along by a light tailwind, flew southwest over the ocean. In midafternoon a surf fisherman stopped casting his lure for a moment to watch Danaus and several other monarchs arrive safely at Island Beach State Park in New Jersey. After the near disaster of the previous day, Danaus had used a day of favorable weather to cross sixty miles of ocean, the most perilous water crossing of her journey.

Next morning a warm breeze blew off the sea. As it struck cooler air along the New Jersey shore, the warm air rose, creating a long thermal along the ocean's edge. Danaus spiraled upward and glided southwest. She seldom needed a full wingbeat, but made continual adjustments of the angle of her body and wings, conserving her energy by using the lifting power of the air. In a few hours she reached the southern tip of New Jersey. Open water lay ahead, and it was time to refuel.

Monarchs gathered at Cape May, waiting for a favorable wind to carry them across Delaware Bay.

That afternoon thousands of monarch butterflies descended on Cape May and clustered on clumps of seaside goldenrod. Like Danaus, many of them were from New England states. Others were from New York, Pennsylvania, and New Jersey and had been blown eastward to the coast, then followed it to Cape May. Naturalists from the Cape May Bird Observatory caught scores of them in butterfly nets. Each butterfly was removed gently from the net, and a lightweight gummed paper tag was stuck to a wing. Then the monarch was let go, bearing a tag with its own identification number and an address. The naturalists made a record of each butterfly tagged: the location, date, condition of the butterfly, and whether it was a male or female. They hoped that someone else would catch the monarch, or at least find it dead, and send information about it to the address on the tag. Each butterfly tagged was a tiny chance of learning more about monarch migration.

Danaus was not tagged. She had glided down a bit inland. She landed on a ten-foot-tall bush festooned with white blossoms. The taste sensors in her middle pair of legs told her that this was a good nectar source. In fact, it was called butterfly bush.

When monarchs settle upon flowers to sip nectar, they are captured for tagging.

This shrub is planted deliberately by many gardeners who live in Cape May. They enjoy the fall spectacle of migratory monarchs, and their gardens feature the kinds of late-blooming flowers that monarchs prefer. Gardeners all over North America are creating butterfly gardens, choosing plants that attract swallowtails, hairstreaks, monarchs, and other

Scooped from a flower by a long-handled net, a monarch is tagged on its right forewing. Some scales are rubbed from the wing surface before the adhesive tag is applied. Each butterfly has its own number and an address for reporting discovery of the butterfly. One male monarch tagged on September 19, 1994, in Cape May, New Jersey, was found dead near Austin, Texas, two months later.

species. The garden where Danaus first tasted butterfly bush was just the first of several butterfly gardens she found on her journey.

That night she slept in a cedar tree with a hundred or more other monarchs. Closer to the shore of Delaware Bay, still other monarchs clustered on bayberry bushes. The morning brought the migrating butterflies an ideal wind: light, from the northeast. Within an hour several thousand monarchs set out across the bay, and every one—including Danaus—safely traversed fifteen miles of water, arriving on the Delaware shore in the early afternoon.

After resting and feeding, many of the monarchs flew south along the Delaware shore. Danaus and others turned more to the west, striking out across Delaware and into eastern Maryland. By accident, Danaus chose a route that took her over mile after mile of forest. She saw no flowers to feed on, and there were no helpful thermals to make her flight easy. It was late afternoon and she felt fam-

North America's monarch migration is one of nature's greatest spectacles, but other butterflies migrate, too. Among the species that cross southern India each year is a butterfly called the Buddha banded peacock. In Costa Rica, monarchs and other butterflies leave the Pacific coast in the dry season and fly through mountain passes to the Atlantic coast. They return to the Pacific zone at the start of the wet season there.

31

ished. She skimmed along just above the treetops, eager to find nectar flowers.

There ahead was an open field, and beyond that a school and houses. There were children on the grassy field, some running and kicking a soccer ball, some standing still, but Danaus paid little attention to them because she had spied two spots of bright orange at one end of the field. Desperately hungry, she sailed down toward one of these flower clusters. A boy and a girl were standing nearby as Danaus prepared to land. Then, just a foot away, she saw that the object was not a stand of the flowers she needed but some bright orange *thing*. She rose quickly.

"Hey, look, a monarch," said Danielle to Kevin. She was playing defender and he was goalie in this practice of their fifth-grade soccer team. The orange objects near them were plastic traffic cones that their coach had set on the ground to serve as temporary goalposts.

Kevin didn't respond, so Danielle said, "That monarch's on its way to Mexico."

"Oh, sure," Kevin scoffed.

"Really. You can look it up in a science book."

"Yeah, a science fiction book."

Danielle gave up and just watched the monarch sail over the low school building. Then the action in the team scrimmage came toward her and she focused on soccer. That night, though, she told her father about the monarch that was fooled by an orange plastic cone.

Beyond the school Danaus found a suburban garden of delights: marigolds, sunflowers, and even some honeysuckle. Rain forced Danaus to stay by that garden, in a pine tree, all of the following day and night. When the weather cleared, she fed, soon rode a thermal nearly a mile high, and had an extraordinary day. She crossed

Chesapeake Bay and the Potomac River, finally gliding down in central Virginia.

As she sipped from a phlox flower the next morning, a hummingbird zoomed into her view and began taking nectar from nearby blossoms. The butterfly and the bird were about the same size. Danaus had seen several hummingbirds in her travels. When this hummingbird moved closer, Danaus was frightened by the intense humming sound and the blurred motion of its rapidly beating wings. She flew to another cluster of flowers.

Often when Danaus rose into the sky, she found herself sharing it with migrating birds. Some were traveling only a few hundred miles, others a thousand miles or more, but they were all flying south. Some flew only at night. Some flew with steady wingbeats at low altitudes, while others, like Danaus, rose in the swirling columns of thermals, then soared southward.

Danaus had become accustomed to seeing fellow migrators—birds and also other monarchs. One day a barn swallow had swooped close to her. Swallows eat small flying insects, but this bird flew off, perhaps because of Danaus's impressive four-inch wingspan.

Flying southwest along the Appalachian Mountains, Danaus encountered hundreds of migrating hawks. Broad-wings and redtails rode the thermals with her, spiraling and soaring a mile above the mountains. A broad-winged hawk fixed its fierce gaze on her as they glided past each other, then continued on its way. Farther along the mountain range, Danaus flew

Gardens that are planted to attract butterflies need at least six hours of sunlight a day. Flowers that butterflies prefer for nectar include aster, cornflower, marigold, strawflower, zinnia, coreopsis, phlox, honeysuckle, and butterfly weed.

33

Many hawks, falcons, eagles, and vultures migrate at the same time as monarch butterflies, and most, like the monarchs, take advantage of the lifting power of warm air. The sun-heated air of a thermal may rise as fast as twenty feet a second.

A group of hawks riding a thermal together is called a kettle. A single kettle may be made of several hundred hawks.

People once thought that monarchs spent winters in hollow trees, or that they migrated no farther than Florida. In 1937 Canadian entomologist Fred Urquhart began putting identification tags on the wings of monarchs. Eventually returns of the tags, plus sightings of masses of monarchs along the Gulf Coast and in Texas and Mexico, led to searches in Mexico. Using information from Urquhart, in 1974 Kenneth Brugger found the first of several sites where millions of monarchs overwinter in central Mexico.

above a bald eagle for a time. The eagle rose from its perch by the shore of a lake and began its ascent on the thermal in which she and several hawks rode. Then the eagle spiraled up out of sight behind Danaus as she glided southwest, waiting to feel the lift of yet another column of warm air rising from a mountain valley.

In southern Kentucky Danaus spied a scattering of orange flowers in a meadow. Soon she was sipping nectar from butterfly weed, a member of the milkweed family. Butterfly weed grows in New England, but Danaus had never tasted it. The plants had stopped blooming before Danaus had emerged from her chrysalis as a butterfly. Now, as she flew farther and farther south, Danaus flew into a warmer climate. She had left autumn and flown into late summer. Still, the late-blooming butterfly weed was a rare treat. Danaus fed mostly on a wealth of sunflowers, thistles, honeysuckle, and other nectar-producing plants.

Whenever she settled down to feed, or to sleep near a nectar source, Danaus was joined by other monarchs from the northeastern United States and from southern Canada. Bit by bit, mile after mile, millions of monarch butterflies were becoming more concentrated as they flew southwest.

Danaus gained about eighty or more miles a day, pausing only to feed or to sit out rainstorms or strong head winds. Even a helping wind, blowing from the northeast, could sometimes be too strong for high flying. In such winds Danaus and the other monarchs usually stayed close to the ground—sometimes a dangerous place for a butterfly.

In Arkansas, east of Little Rock, Danaus and other monarchs were kept low by a gusty wind from the north. They had crossed the Mississippi River the day before. Still heading southwest, Danaus flew across a field, staying just above the plant stems. She passed over a fence and a ditch, then began to cross a clear space: Interstate Highway 40.

Suddenly a huge *something* rushed toward her. Danaus beat her wings in a frantic effort to rise. She just missed smashing into a glass surface, then was flung over the back of the giant thing. She struggled to right herself in the violent eddies of wind left behind while it rushed on. Danaus was unhurt. She flew higher and crossed the rest of the highway. The car, now a mile away, had a monarch butterfly stuck in an opening by a headlight, and another wedged against a windshield wiper. On this windy day in Arkansas, scores of low-flying monarchs would end their journeys—and their lives—in this way.

Days of warm weather with light winds followed, bringing Danaus to central Texas. The land grew more and more arid. Nectar flowers were hard to find in the desert. Danaus found food near streams where the water sustained not only willow and cypress trees to rest in but also frostweed. This three-foot-high plant produced clusters of white blossoms like miniature sunflowers. And every-where frostweed grew, in wet spots and in the shade of oaks, mon-archs descended to feed.

Danaus spent five days in a small canyon near Eagle Pass, a few miles from the Rio Grande and Mexico. It was hot, almost ninety degrees Fahrenheit. She rested in shady places and sipped frostweed nectar. Much of the food energy that she took in was stored in her

The brilliant white flowers of frostweed are a vital source of food as monarchs reach the last leg of their journey.

body as fat. Wherever she went, she met hundreds of other monarchs, a tiny fraction of the millions that, like Danaus, were feasting and waiting for something.

A bit of information in the ganglia of these monarchs told them all to wait. Then one day their wait was over. A cold front swept across the Southwest, bringing cooler weather and winds from the north. Danaus sensed the change and rose from her last meal of Texas frostweed, flying up, up, and south into Mexico. The sky was full of monarchs. Within a few hours none could be found in the shady Texas canyons.

Danaus took advantage of thermals and the wind and, using all of her flying skills, traveled deeper and deeper into Mexico. From a hayfield in Massachusetts she had flown two thousand miles and crossed most of a continent. Now bits of information in her ganglion, the butterfly wisdom that had brought her this far, told her that her journey was nearly over.

OPPOSITE: *Danaus paused in a Texas canyon. She feasted on frostweed flowers and awaited the winds that would carry her deep into Mexico.*

To a Mountain in Mexico

BROAD RIVERS OF MONARCH butterflies flowed from Texas into Mexico, then spread out as they traveled south. Back in central Texas new arrivals massed and waited for the next cold front from the north. Meanwhile, streams of monarchs numbering in the tens of millions flew along the Gulf Coast, then struck inland across Mexico. Within a few weeks more than a hundred million monarchs would reach their destination: the forested high peaks in volcanic mountain ranges west of Mexico City.

This vast mountainous area in central Mexico is called the Transverse Neovolcanic Belt. About thirty million years ago this landscape shook, rumbled, and smoked with erupting volcanoes. Now the lava beds, cinder cones, and other remains of those volcanoes are mostly cloaked in green meadows and forests. Just twelve thousand years ago, when glaciers covered much of northern North America, evergreen forests flourished on the lower slopes of the

From October 31 through November 2, Mexicans celebrate the Days of the Dead—holidays that honor the memory of relatives and friends who have died. At the same time, millions of monarca mariposas—monarch butterflies—are arriving in central Mexico. According to ancient myth, the monarchs represent the returning souls of the dead.

39

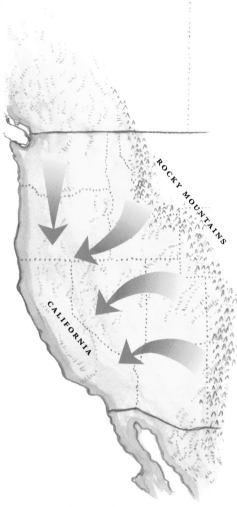

Monarchs west of the Rocky Mountains migrate toward the Pacific. Some in Arizona fly northwest to overwintering sites. The butterflies find the cool climate they need in groves of trees within a half mile of the coast. There are more than 120 sites, all in California except for one in northern Mexico. Some overwintering sites have been destroyed or damaged, but efforts are being made to save those that remain.

mountains in central Mexico. Then the earth's climate warmed. Trees and other plants that had thrived in a cold climate were replaced by other species. Today just a few kinds of cold-climate plants still survive high in the mountains, between nine and twelve thousand feet above sea level. One survivor is the oyamel fir, an evergreen tree that sometimes reaches 150 feet in height.

As dawn sunlight reached out to touch Danaus, she clung to a bough of an oyamel fir. The day before, as she flew south through a mountain pass, she had seen a column of monarchs rising above a ridge. They circled higher and higher, and this towering display lured Danaus and countless other monarchs to join the group over the ridge. When the monarchs descended in the late afternoon, they glided down to fir trees below the ridge. Danaus shared a fir tree with thousands of other monarchs and the nearby fir forest with monarchs that numbered in the millions.

There were other tall trees in the forest—pines and cypress—and also young trees and shrubs, including oak, alder, willow, and madrone. Still, the whole environment was dramatically unlike Danaus's birthplace in Massachusetts and the continent she had crossed to reach this stand of fir trees.

The position of the sun in the sky, the thin air at this high altitude, the scent molecules carried to her antennae by the wind—so much was new and foreign. She had never been in Mexico before. Neither had her parents, grandparents, or great-grandparents. Nevertheless, Danaus must have felt at home. Wisdom passed down from generations of monarchs, stored in her ganglion, had guided her to a mountain in Mexico that would be her home for nearly half of her life.

Monarchs from all over the central and eastern United States and parts of southeastern Canada had reached their winter homes in

proboscis

a high-peaks area of the Transverse Neovolcanic Belt that measured seventy-five by thirty-five miles. Their actual refuges were a small part of this region. As November's days grew shorter and the nights grew colder, the monarchs became more concentrated. Small groups joined others and formed larger groups. The monarchs rested close together, side by side, wings often touching, clinging to firs and other trees in just a dozen sites, each a few acres in size. Some of the monarchs near Danaus had been born in the Midwest. Others were from Georgia, Pennsylvania, New Jersey. Danaus had flown nearly three thousand miles in about a month's time. Some monarchs resting in the fir trees had traveled even farther—from Maine and other states of northern New England, and from southern Canada.

Remarkably, none of the butterflies looked as if they had just completed a great journey. Aside from the notch ripped in her wing by the cat's claw on Long Island, Danaus looked as fit and pretty as the day she first took flight. All of the monarchs were still brightly colored. Their abdomens were plump with stored fat. With the help of energy-saving winds and thermals, plus the nectar of thousands of flowers—especially the frostweeds of Texas and northern Mexico—most of the butterflies had actually gained weight during their migration.

Danaus spent the whole day on the fir bough, scarcely moving. Sunlight touched her body and wings but warmed her slowly in the chilly mountain air, two miles above sea level. All of the monarchs rested with wings folded flat. From a distance the butterflies looked like masses of dead leaves or brown drapes hung upon the trees.

The next day was warmer. After spreading her wings and basking in the sun for a few minutes, Danaus flew down the mountain slope to a ravine where sunlight sparkled from a stream. She landed on a stone by the water's edge and took a drink. Many monarchs

A monarch's proboscis is tightly coiled until the butterfly drinks. Uncoiled, it is half the length of the monarch's body.

OVERLEAF: *After basking in the morning sun, thousands of monarchs warm their wing muscles enough to fly in search of water.*

proboscis

Monarchs need water in order to survive in good health until spring. They line the edges of ponds, puddles, and even little trickling streams, sipping water.

were doing the same. Others flew downslope and sipped nectar from little sunflowers that grew wild in fields and along roads. Later in the afternoon they all returned to the fir forest and settled in. Night came a bit earlier than the day before.

A few last straggling monarchs joined Danaus's colony. As December advanced, the days and nights grew colder. The monarch colony moved southwest down the mountain slope, away from the ridge. One night a storm struck the ridge, coating every branch of the forest there with ice. Although Danaus and the other monarchs were just a quarter mile away, they were at a lower elevation and in a valley where the climate around them was milder. They endured a cold, wet, windy night but were spared catastrophe. Often the temperature stayed well below fifty-five degrees Fahrenheit for several days in a row. None of the monarchs took flight. They clung to twigs, fir needles, and tree trunks, resting and conserving energy.

A warm day dawned. The monarchs basked in the sun until their wing muscles absorbed enough warmth, then rose into the sky. They seemed to revel in the chance to flap their wings and soar. They glided downslope, settling beside streams for a drink. Then, as daylight grew faint, the monarchs flew up the slope to the fir forest. They settled down, as usual avoiding the treetops—the windiest and coldest zone of their refuge. They also avoided the lowest parts of trees and bushes. Somehow they sensed that there was danger near the forest floor.

Danaus landed on a pine bough, joining thousands of other monarchs already clinging to the needles. The bough bent under the weight of several pounds of butterflies. That night a cold wind buffeted the forest. Danaus felt the pine bough sway beneath her feet. Then a gust of wind interrupted the movement.

With a sharp crack the bough broke and fell. Some monarchs fluttered off and managed to catch hold of other branches. Danaus and thousands of other monarchs still clung to the bough when it crashed to the forest floor. Some were crushed and killed. Most of the butterflies, Danaus among them, were flung free by the impact and fell onto the mossy ground.

It was dark and cold. Many monarchs lay where they fell. Their body temperatures were so low that they could not move. They were helpless. Danaus and a few others still retained a bit of warmth from their day in the bright sunshine. Shivering and flexing their wings—actions that helped warm their bodies—they spread out over the moss, searching for something to climb.

There was no moon, but light from stars, so bright in the clear mountain air, revealed faint shapes in the forest. Danaus searched for some vertical form, any small or large stem. As she crawled slowly along, she sensed shapes moving over the forest floor—monarchs and other things: mice. Every night in the mountains, black-eared mice emerged from hiding places to search the forest for food. Ordinarily they ate mostly seeds and berries. But here, on the forest floor beneath a winter monarch colony, they also ate butterflies.

Black-eared mice feast on monarchs. They may be less sensitive than other predators to the bitter taste of the butterflies.

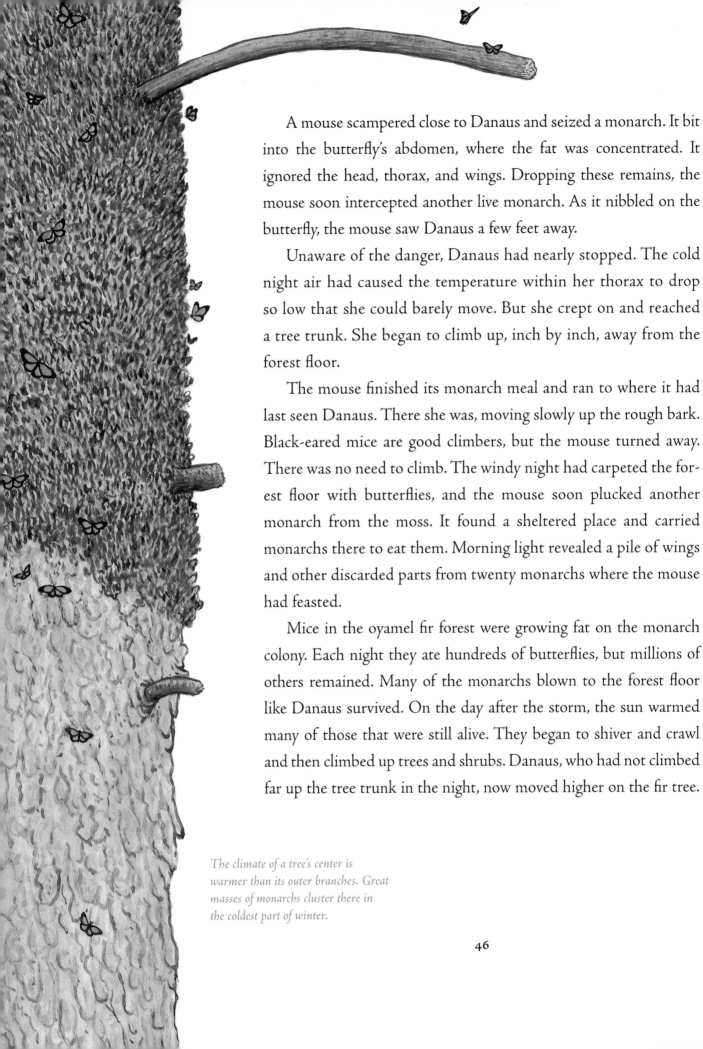

A mouse scampered close to Danaus and seized a monarch. It bit into the butterfly's abdomen, where the fat was concentrated. It ignored the head, thorax, and wings. Dropping these remains, the mouse soon intercepted another live monarch. As it nibbled on the butterfly, the mouse saw Danaus a few feet away.

Unaware of the danger, Danaus had nearly stopped. The cold night air had caused the temperature within her thorax to drop so low that she could barely move. But she crept on and reached a tree trunk. She began to climb up, inch by inch, away from the forest floor.

The mouse finished its monarch meal and ran to where it had last seen Danaus. There she was, moving slowly up the rough bark. Black-eared mice are good climbers, but the mouse turned away. There was no need to climb. The windy night had carpeted the forest floor with butterflies, and the mouse soon plucked another monarch from the moss. It found a sheltered place and carried monarchs there to eat them. Morning light revealed a pile of wings and other discarded parts from twenty monarchs where the mouse had feasted.

Mice in the oyamel fir forest were growing fat on the monarch colony. Each night they ate hundreds of butterflies, but millions of others remained. Many of the monarchs blown to the forest floor like Danaus survived. On the day after the storm, the sun warmed many of those that were still alive. They began to shiver and crawl and then climbed up trees and shrubs. Danaus, who had not climbed far up the tree trunk in the night, now moved higher on the fir tree.

The climate of a tree's center is warmer than its outer branches. Great masses of monarchs cluster there in the coldest part of winter.

In January, the heart of winter, temperatures dropped close to freezing in the monarch colony. Some butterflies died. The survivors moved inward on the trees, becoming more concentrated on main branches and trunks, which were more sheltered from the cold than outer small branches and fir needles. Somehow the monarchs sensed this small difference in climate (a microclimate). They took advantage of it, and it helped many of them survive.

Although January was the coldest month in the mountains, each day was a little longer. Late in the month there were some warm spells, a hint of spring. Often many days passed without rain. Winter was the dry season in the mountains. Whenever the monarchs felt warm enough to fly, they glided downslope to drink water. They relied on their stored fat as a source of energy but had to replenish the fluids in their bodies.

Steller's jays and most other insect-eating birds of central Mexico's mountains occasionally eat monarchs.

One afternoon, after a drink, Danaus flew up the mountain slope and approached the grove of firs where her colony had stayed for several days. Many butterflies lingered in the warm air above the trees. They seemed reluctant to take refuge, perhaps sensing an approaching cold front. When Danaus finally settled down, she chose to rest on a bough high in the canopy of a fir tree. Until now she had usually roosted lower in trees, closer to the ground.

By accident she put herself in danger—not from the cold weather that arrived overnight, but from predatory birds that often hunted for butterflies on cold days. In order to survive the low temperatures, the birds needed extra energy and they found it in the plump bodies of the monarchs. Earlier in the winter, Danaus had seen a small flock of Steller's jays flash by her resting place, grabbing monarchs as they passed quickly through the fir forest. This time, in the chill morning air, a large flock of black-headed grosbeaks and black-backed orioles descended on the forest. Monarch butterflies are an important winter food source for these birds. Several dozen grosbeaks and orioles flew into the forest canopy and began plucking butterflies from their resting sites. Soon a shower of discarded wings and other monarch body parts began to fall to the forest floor—already carpeted with the remains of butterflies killed by cold, wind, and mice.

Each species of bird had its special way of eating. The grosbeaks snapped off whole monarch abdomens, eating not just the stored fat within but also the exoskeletons. The orioles pierced monarchs' abdomens and thoraxes with their sharp beaks, then plucked out fat and muscles, eating very little of the exoskeletons. Neither species ate wings, where the concentration of milkweed poisons was greatest.

After eating their fill, the birds flew off, but they returned in the afternoon. A pair of orioles landed abruptly on the bough where Danaus clung, dislodging some monarchs, plucking others with their beaks. One oriole advanced toward Danaus. It expertly held a monarch down with one claw, then ripped a slit in its abdomen and ate the contents. The oriole lifted its head, saw Danaus, and stepped toward her.

Danaus was cold. She could not muster the energy for a single wingbeat. She took the only action she could: she let go with her feet and fell. She plummeted with wings closed and landed on moss. Danaus righted herself and began to shiver. After warming up a bit, she walked to a pine tree and began to climb. From that day on she rested in the lower parts of trees, where orioles and grosbeaks rarely hunted.

In the following weeks the days grew longer, the sunlight stronger. Daytime temperatures sometimes reached sixty degrees. It was mid-February—not spring on a calendar, but becoming springlike in the mountains of central Mexico.

Throughout the oyamel fir forests, countless millions of mon-

On cold days black-headed grosbeaks and orioles eat many monarchs. Sometimes the poison within the monarchs causes the birds to sicken. They hunt other food for a few days, then return to feast on more butterflies.

black-headed grosbeak

archs had died in their winter refuges. At one site orioles and grosbeaks killed more than two million monarchs, nearly a tenth of the butterflies in the colony. Others died as a result of the rugged high-altitude climate. Most monarchs survived, however, because of that very same climate.

black-backed oriole

Rugged though it was, the climate was ideal for the monarchs. They needed to conserve energy through the winter for mating and their return migration in the spring. They used little energy because the cold climate kept them inactive, yet the microclimate of the fir forests usually protected them from the most severe temperatures. And even though winter was the dry season, there was enough moisture from clouds that enshrouded the mountains, from dew, from rainfall, and from streams, to provide water that the monarchs needed. Actually, a climate with more rain would have harmed the monarchs' chances for survival, since they freeze more readily at low temperatures when they get wet.

The climate north and south of the Transverse Neovolcanic Belt offers no winter refuge for monarchs. South lies the dry, hot Balsas River valley. North lie plains whose climate is colder and drier than that of the mountains—a climate where no monarch could survive. In the mountainous fir forests of Mexico the monarchs had found the ideal place—and apparently the only place—to survive the winter.

Now spring approached. Danaus and the other butterflies were about to begin the last great adventure of their lives.

An Extraordinary Life

I**N LATE FEBRUARY** there was a sound in the fir forest like leaves rustling in a strong breeze. It was a windless day, however, and the sound came from the wings of millions of monarch butterflies, beginning to flutter free of their winter home.

Some of them would return later in the day after gliding downslope to sip nectar from spring wildflowers that were now blooming all over the lower elevations in the mountains. And some of the returning monarchs would stop a bit short of the main group, clustering together in a separate part of the forest. The winter colony was beginning to break up. Danaus, however, was still part of the main group, which, despite winter losses, numbered over ten million monarchs.

Lengthening days and warm temperatures brought change to the oyamel fir forest. The air was filled with spring songs of flycatchers and other birds—and with the smell of decaying butterfly remains on the forest floor. The most remarkable change of all, however, was

The monarch butterfly, a native North American species for at least two million years, has been nominated as the national insect of the United States. Its chief rival for this honor is the honeybee, an insect that originated in Asia or Africa and was first brought to North America in 1621 by European colonists.

51

in the monarchs themselves. Late last summer, when they had first emerged as butterflies, the shortening days that had signaled the approach of autumn had halted development of their reproductive systems. Now each day was a bit longer than the day before—a sign of approaching spring and a stimulus that prepared the monarchs for the mating season.

Many of the butterflies had used up a lot of their stored fat. They had lost weight, though their colors were still bright. More important than their looks, however, were changes within their bodies. Of course, not all of the monarchs were ready to mate at the same time. Furthermore, the males did all of the courting and the females were often uninterested. One day a male monarch landed beside Danaus. She sensed an unusual odor wafting from the scent glands on his hind wings. He stroked her head and thorax with his antennae. Danaus flew away, zigzagging through tree branches, and eluded the pursuing male.

Some monarchs mated on the ground or on leaves or other vegetation. Many met in the air above the forest and surrounding land. Each day a skyful of monarchs became more frenzied as males chased females (and sometimes other males), some females tried to evade males, and some males and females joined to mate. Sometimes a female that was receptive to a male's interest would spiral slowly down to the ground with the male following her. More often a male would catch a female in the air and bring her to earth. This is what happened to Danaus.

Gliding above the forest, she saw a small male monarch flying rapidly toward her. She began to zig and zag, but the male flew directly above her and grasped her wings with his feet. Then he closed his wings. Danaus could not carry his weight. They tumbled down to the mossy ground.

Sometimes a male monarch courts a female by rubbing his antennae on her head and thorax.

Again Danaus smelled the unusual scent given off by the male. She found the aroma alluring. The male pressed the tip of his abdomen against hers and grasped it with organs called claspers. Danaus and the male stayed joined by their abdomens for several hours, and during this time he passed a packet containing sperm (called a spermatophore) into a special organ within her abdomen. Then they parted.

During the following week, Danaus mated with other males. Each time she gained sperm that would fertilize the several hundred eggs that had begun to develop within her. She also gained something more: fat and other nutrients that were part of the spermatophores. One nutrient, protein, was especially important in the development of her eggs. Within a few hours of mating, the remains of the spermatophore packets broke down and added to Danaus's energy reserves. Any new source of energy was welcome. The winter had reduced her fat supplies, and the frenzy of the mating season had depleted them further. She would soon need every bit of energy she could muster.

One morning in late March Danaus gave her wings a powerful downbeat and lifted off her perch on an oyamel fir. She rose through the air and flew northeast and downslope, heading toward a valley she had last seen in early November. She didn't look back at the spiraling, darting, tumbling cloud of monarchs behind her. And the nerve cells in her ganglion were much too simple for her to think about how she was leaving her winter home or to feel regret about leaving forever the special environment of the mountain fir forests. For Danaus the strong drive to mate was being replaced by another powerful urge: to fly north and find milkweed plants on which to lay her eggs.

Millions of monarchs, both females and males, streamed north.

The act of mating makes possible a new generation of monarchs and also gives females nutrients that are vital for the development of their eggs.

Hurrying northward, the monarchs that survived winter are near the end of their lives. Their colors fade; their wings are often tattered.

Beyond the Transverse Neovolcanic Belt they spread out, breaking into small groups or flying alone over the plains. When females paused to sip nectar from wildflowers, they were sometimes courted by males. Mating still occurred. The females set the pace northward, with the males in pursuit. When the opportunity of a thermal or a light tailwind arose, the butterflies soared high and glided along effortlessly. When the winds were not favorable, however, the female monarchs did not rest. They raced onward, aiming to find milkweeds hundreds of miles to the north.

Within a few days Danaus passed from Mexico into Texas. Daytime temperatures sometimes reached eighty degrees. The warmth speeded up the development of the eggs within her, though they were not all maturing at the same pace. She flew on. Traveling in the hot weather took a toll on Danaus. She lost weight. The bright orange and black of her upper wings began to fade. She was aging. Like her mother, once she had mated she had only a few weeks more to live.

Danaus saw fewer and fewer monarchs, though millions of them were fanning out across northern Mexico, Texas, and Louisiana.

There was no advantage in migrating in groups. The first milkweeds of spring could sprout almost anywhere, so each female monarch was on her own personal quest.

Danaus passed south of Dallas, Texas, in early April. Each day she fluttered along, just a few feet above the ground, searching for milkweed in likely-looking meadows or roadside patches of dried weed stems. She sometimes took nectar from flowers but mostly just paused long enough to look—and smell—for milkweed. Nothing so far.

Her first batch of eggs was well developed and added to her weight. Danaus became almost frantic with her desire to find the milkweed her young would need to eat. She flew on, using up more and more of her dwindling store of energy.

Then, at last, on a south-facing slope in northeast Texas, close to the Arkansas border, she found what she had hunted for: milkweed. The stems had sprouted from the soil just a few days before, but already tender new leaves were unfolding in the sunshine. Danaus wasted no time. She swung under a leaf and pressed the tip of her abdomen to its surface. Her very first tiny egg squeezed out and

Most scientists believe that the extraordinary migration of monarch butterflies began nearly two million years ago. Glacial periods caused the range of both monarchs and milkweeds to retreat southward. The present long-range migration began about ten thousand years ago, when vast glaciers retreated northward. As the climate warmed, milkweed spread northward and monarchs followed, pursuing their summer food source.

stuck to the leaf. She flew to another milkweed, then another, depositing eggs.

Twilight forced her to stop. She slept near the place where her firstborn young would feed and develop into butterflies themselves. The next morning she flew on. Her remaining eggs were maturing quickly in the warm weather. Danaus found sweet nectar flowers and sometimes paused to feed. Her search for milkweed continued.

In the next two days Danaus found more milkweed and laid more eggs. Then, just over the Arkansas border, she discovered a large pasture studded with fresh new milkweed plants. There she laid the last of her eggs, which had numbered almost five hundred in all.

The field resembled the hayfield in Massachusetts where—seven months ago—Danaus had emerged from an egg herself as a tiny caterpillar. Already, back in Texas, her own young were now rasping their way out of their eggs, crawling out and taking their own first bites of milkweed. Soon they would be strong young butterflies, eager to mate and to fly northeast. Later in the spring some of them, or perhaps their young, would glide down from the sky and sip nectar and gather near patches of milkweed in Massachusetts, or beyond. And in the fall, descendants of Danaus would spiral high in thermals and set out for Mexico.

After depositing her last egg, Danaus flew to a nearby clover blossom. She had barely enough energy to sip some nectar. Danaus was tired and bedraggled. The food might sustain her for another day or two. Then, like every other monarch of the spring, her life would be over.

It had been a life of adventure. Danaus had made a great journey, faced many dangers, and helped create a new generation of monarch butterflies. She had lived an extraordinary life.

Monarch migration, including the butterflies' return in the spring, still holds many mysteries. Volunteers, young and old, help find clues by tagging monarchs and by simply observing and reporting compass readings of monarchs in flight. For information about this research, write to: Monarch Watch, Dept. of Entomology, 7005 Haworth Hall, University of Kansas, Lawrence, KS 66045.
e-mail: monarch@falcon.cc.ukans.edu
http://monarch.bio.ukans.edu

Saving the Monarchs' Winter Refuges

THE MIGRATION of monarch butterflies—one of the most extraordinary phenomena in all of nature—depends on the existence of the special forested sites where the butterflies rest in the winter. If all of these refuges were destroyed, some nonmigratory populations of monarchs would remain (for example, in Florida and Central America), but monarchs would no longer brighten the summer fields and gardens of most of the United States or of Canada.

West of the Rocky Mountains, monarchs fly each autumn to more than 120 overwintering sites scattered along 620 miles of the California coast. The numbers of butterflies at each site are much smaller than in the Mexican mountains; they range from dozens to about one hundred thousand. Most of the sites occur within a half mile of the seashore—land that is highly prized for homes, motels, and resorts. At least thirty sites have been, or are being, destroyed.

Some monarch overwintering sites are now protected by law. A bond act approved by California voters in 1988 provided $2 million for buying some sites outright. Others have become refuges, thanks to agreements in which landowners promise not to disturb any portion of their property where monarchs gather. Such agreements, called conservation easements, are a vital part of the effort to ensure survival of the western monarch butterfly migration.

In California, the Xerces Society played a key role in gaining protection of some monarch overwintering sites. It sells a sixteen-page booklet, *The Monarch Habitat Handbook*, which gives details about protecting overwintering habitats in California. For information, write to The Xerces Society, 4828 Southeast Hawthorne Blvd., Portland, OR 97215.

In Mexico many millions of butterflies are clustered at just a dozen sites. The winter survival of all of these monarchs that migrate from the United States and Canada east of the Rockies depends on protection of high-altitude oyamel fir forests. Only about 100,000 to 125,000 acres of this habitat remain.

The forests where monarchs gather are owned by local communities that are not allowed to sell the land. As populations have grown, forests have been cleared for agriculture. Trees are also sold to lumber companies or used by local residents for fuel and for home building. Just removing a few large trees from the core of a monarch overwintering site can do great harm; their loss can affect the special winter microclimate that the butterflies need for survival.

In 1986 the Mexican government took steps to protect five overwintering areas, but some tree cutting has continued; one refuge has been nearly destroyed. The nearby communities are poor; people are trying to scrape a living from the land. The challenge is to convince them that they will benefit from protecting the fir forests. At two refuges that are open to the public, local people do earn income by serving as guides and by selling food, T-shirts, and souvenirs to tourists.

The Mexican overwintering sites where millions of monarchs gather are in grave danger. For more information about these refuges and how you can help gain their protection, write to Monarch Butterfly Program, The Wildlife Conservation Society, New York Zoological Society, Bronx Park, New York, NY 10460.

Monarch winter colonies in Mexico

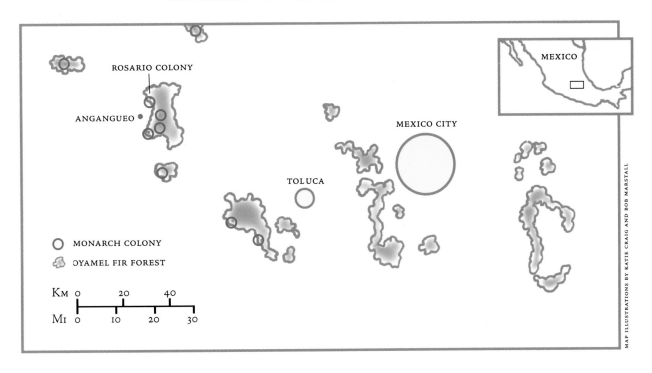

How To Raise Monarch Butterflies

IN MOST of the United States and southern Canada, you can raise some monarch butterflies, then let them fly away. By following the instructions on these pages, you can get a close-up view as a monarch caterpillar feeds, forms its chrysalis, and later emerges as a butterfly, right in your own home or school.

Before you begin, be sure you have a handy supply of milkweed plants that will provide the leaves that the caterpillars will need for food. Also, prepare a home for the caterpillars. A ten-gallon glass or plastic aquarium with a screen top is a good container in which to raise a few monarchs.

You can collect and carry the caterpillars in a large glass or plastic jar, or even in a gallon-size plastic bag. (Don't leave the container in direct sunshine, or solar heat will kill the caterpillars.) You may find the distinctive-looking monarch caterpillars wherever milkweed grows, but they are usually most plentiful in a patch of milkweed plants that were cut earlier in the summer and then resprouted. Besides looking on the undersides of leaves for the caterpillars themselves, watch for signs of their presence: marks left by

their chewing on leaves, and little lumps of dark-green or black frass (their droppings).

The caterpillars do not bite. As you gently pick up a few with your fingers, also collect some milkweed stalks for their food. Break the stalks off at ground level. Back home, bend the bottoms of the stalks so that they lean upright against the sides of the aquarium or other container. DO NOT set the ends of the stalks in water; they do not absorb water well, and caterpillars may drown in the water container. To help keep the milkweed fresh, keep the container's air somewhat humid by covering most of the screen top with glass, plastic, or plastic wrap. However, if water vapor drops form inside the container, the air is too humid. Adjust the cover to let some moisture escape. Every two or three days remove the milkweed and replace it with freshly picked stalks. At the same time clean the frass from the caterpillars' home.

Watch for telltale signs that a caterpillar is about to form its chrysalis. It will hang upside down in a J shape, from a milkweed leaf or stem but more likely from the screen. It will hang like this for a day or two. Watch the filaments by its head. Within half an hour after they collapse, the caterpillar's exoskeleton will be shed. If for any reason a chrysalis comes loose from its hanging place, you can attach its stalk to the screen with a piece of thread.

Sometimes a monarch chrysalis does not produce a butterfly because a parasite, a tachina fly, laid one or more eggs on the monarch caterpillar. The eggs develop into white maggots that chew their way out of the chrysalis, then drop on slime threads to the floor of the container where each soon forms a dark brown pupa. If you leave the pupa alone, a hairy-looking adult tachina fly will emerge from it in about two weeks.

Normally, however, in about ten days (the range is from five to fifteen) a monarch butterfly will be ready to emerge from its chrysalis. Watch for the darkening of the chrysalis, when you can see the color pattern of the butterfly's wings. Check the chrysalis frequently so that you do not miss the moment a butterfly emerges. Many monarchs emerge in the morning, around 9:00 to 10:00 A.M. If the weather is sunny and warm, let the butterfly go soon after its wings have hardened (a process that takes at least two hours). If the weather is cold or rainy, wait for favorable conditions and offer the monarch some sugar water. If this "nectar" is put in a bottle cap or other small container that is brightly colored, the butterfly may be attracted to it. If not, use a toothpick or needle to gently uncoil the monarch's proboscis so that its tip touches the sweet fluid; this usually induces the butterfly to begin feeding.

Let the monarchs go as soon as possible after their wings have hardened. The sooner they are outdoors, flying and seeking flower nectar on their own, the better their chances of surviving, mating, and producing a new generation of monarch butterflies.

Further Reading

The single most valuable source on this subject is *Biology and Conservation of the Monarch Butterfly*, edited by Stephen Malcolm and Myron Zalucki. Published in 1993 by the Natural History Museum of Los Angeles County, it contains more than forty research reports by scientists and others involved in the study of monarch butterflies and their conservation. Several reports from it are among the titles cited below.

Brower, Lincoln P. "Monarch Butterfly Orientation: Missing Pieces of a Magnificent Puzzle." *The Journal of Experimental Biology* 199, no. 1 (1996): 93–106.

———. "Monarch Migration." *Natural History*, June–July 1977: 40–53.

———. "Understanding and Misunderstanding the Migration of the Monarch Butterfly in North America: 1857–1995." *Journal of the Lepidopterists' Society*, December 1995: 304–385.

———, et al. "Mice as Predators of Overwintering Monarch Butterflies in Mexico." *Biotropica*, June 1985: 89–99.

Calvert, William, et al. "The Effect of Rain, Snow, and Freezing Temperatures on Overwintering Monarch Butterflies in Mexico." *Biotropica*, March 1983: 42–47.

Cockrell, Barbara, et al. "Time, Temperature, and Latitudinal Constraints on the Annual Recolonization of Eastern North America by the Monarch Butterfly." In *Biology and Conservation of the Monarch Butterfly*: 233–251.

Herberman, Ethan. *The Great Butterfly Hunt: The Mystery of the Migrating Monarchs*. New York: Simon and Schuster, 1990.

————. "How to Feed a Visiting Monarch: and Other Native Butterflies That You Can Attract to Your Garden." *National Wildlife,* August–September 1994: 14–21.

Lane, John. "Overwintering Monarch Butterflies in California." In *Biology and Conservation of the Monarch Butterfly*: 335–344.

Lasky, Kathryn. *Monarchs.* San Diego: Harcourt Brace, 1993.

Malcolm, Stephen. "Conservation of Monarch Butterfly Migration in North America." In *Biology and Conservation of the Monarch Butterfly*: 357–361.

Snook, Laura. "Conservation of the Monarch Butterfly Reserves in Mexico: Focus on the Forest." In *Biology and Conservation of the Monarch Butterfly*: 363–375.

Urquhart, Fred. "Found at Last: The Monarch's Winter Home." *National Geographic,* August 1976: 160–173.

————. *The Monarch Butterfly: International Traveler.* Chicago: Nelson-Hall, 1987.

Xerces Society, in association with the Smithsonian Institution. *Butterfly Gardening: Creating Summer Magic in Your Garden.* San Francisco: Sierra Club, 1990.

Zalucki, Myron. "Sex Around the Milkweed Patch: The Significance of Patches of Host Plants in Monarch Reproduction." In *Biology and Conservation of the Monarch Butterfly*: 69–76.

Index